A New True Book

THE CIRCUS

By Mabel Harmer

*This "true book" was prepared
under the direction of
Illa Podendorf,
formerly with the Laboratory School,
University of Chicago*

CHILDRENS PRESS, CHICAGO

Circus wagon

Library of Congress Cataloging in Publication Data

Harmer, Mabel, 1894-
The circus.
  (A New true book)
  Previously published as: The true book of the circus. 1955.
  Summary: A brief account of circus life as
the circus moves from town to town and all
prepare for the next show.
  1. Circus—Juvenile literature. [1.   Circus]
I. Title.
GV1817.H37   1981   791.3   81-7709
ISBN 0-516-01610-5   AACR2

TABLE OF CONTENTS

The Show on the Road. . . 5

Circuses With Tents. . . 11

Circus Animals. . . 17

Under the Big Top. . . 25

Circuses Without Tents. . . 29

Show Time. . . 33

Between Shows. . . 42

Words You Should Know. . . 46

Index. . . 47

Some circuses move by truck.

THE SHOW ON THE ROAD

A circus moves from town to town.

Often a circus goes by truck. Tents are loaded on trucks. Animal cages are put on trucks.

The circus people follow the trucks. They ride in motor homes and cars.

A camel comes off a circus train.

A circus can also travel by train. Once, all circuses used trains. Two or three long trains were used to carry everything.

The circus would parade from the train. It went through a town. A band played. Elephants walked by. Lions roared from cages. Then the circus would go to its tents in an open field.

A side show wagon

A modern circus parade

A Big Top tent

Workers and an elephant put up a tent.

CIRCUSES WITH TENTS

Today many circuses use tents. But some are held inside buildings, too.

A circus with tents must put up tents in every town. People and machines do the work. Elephants can help, too.

The cookhouse tent is the first tent to go up. Meals are served in the cook house. The food is cooked in a kitchen on a truck.

Cookhouse wagons

13

As other tents are put up, the animals are taken out of the trucks. Camels, giraffes, and zebras are led to one place.

Some animals of the circus:
zebra (top), llama (middle left),
giraffe (above), elephants (left)

Tigers

CIRCUS ANIMALS

Wild animals are in cages on the trucks. The sides of the trucks are rolled up. Then the cages can be seen.

Lions, tigers, and leopards are wild animals. They are called big cats.

The lion is the most easily trained.

The tiger can learn more tricks than a lion. But a tiger is more dangerous than a lion.

The leopard is the most dangerous of all.

Panthers and leopards

Lions and tigers

Horses are also stars of the show. They carry trick riders. They wear feathers and shiny decorations. They even perform tricks themselves.

Elephants are important circus animals. They can learn many tricks, too.

UNDER THE BIG TOP

The Big Top is the last tent to go up. Here the show will take place.

Inside the Big Top seats are put in place. "Tightrope" wires are strung. Lights are put up. The workers build a circus city.

Miles of rope are used by a circus. New rope is used each year. Good strong rope helps keep performers safe.

MEZ
MEZ
MEZ H
MEZ G
MEZ F
MEZ E

1

28

CIRCUSES WITHOUT TENTS

Circuses that take place inside buildings don't have tents to put up. And seats are already there.

But the workers must also put up tightrope wires and poles. They set up rings. The people and animals perform their acts inside these rings.

SHOW TIME

At last it is time for the show.

People come in and sit down. The band is playing.

The band is the clock of the circus. The music tells the performers how much time they have for each act.

The show opens with a big parade.

Then the acts begin in
the rings. Sometimes two
or three acts go on at the
same time.

A lion tamer works with
the big cats.

Horses and elephants do
tricks with their riders.

Other circus stars work
high above the crowd.
They walk on the
tightropes or swing on
bars held by wires.

Emmett Kelly and Jack LeClair   Modern clowns

The clowns are everywhere.

The performers wait for
their turns to do their acts.

After every show the
tents and the seats are
cleaned.

The next day they do
the show all over again.
More people come to see it.

Being clean helps the elephants stay healthy.

BETWEEN SHOWS

All the circus workers help feed and clean the animals.

A circus doctor tries to keep the animals well. The doctor also takes care of sick animals.

The circus people live in
motor homes or trailers.
Some even share a home
in a large truck. Others
stay in hotels.

In the fall the circus stops going from town to town. It goes to its winter home.

In the winter the circus stars learn new acts. Animals learn new tricks. Everything is painted and cleaned.

And in the spring the circus is ready to go again.

WORDS YOU SHOULD KNOW

act — a performance

area (AYR•ee•uh) — space; a section of land

dangerous (DAYN•jer•us) — not safe; likely to cause harm

decoration (dek•or•AY•shun) — to put on something pretty

hotel (hoh•TELL) — a place to stay when you are away from home

load (LOHD) — to put something to be carried in or on a truck or other vehicle

motor home (MOH•ter hohm) — a house on wheels that can be driven from place to place

parade (puh•RAYD) — to pass before groups of people

perform — to sing, dance, act, and do other things that people can watch

ring — a circle in which circus acts are done

tamer (TAY•mer) — a person who works in a circus with wild animals

tent — a cloth shelter held up with poles and ropes

tightrope wire — a rope or wire pulled tight high over the ground on which circus acts are done

trailer (TRAY•ler) — a large van which can be pulled by a car or truck and used as a house

train (TRAYN) — to teach an animal to perform

trick rider (TRIK RY•der) — a person who does stunts while riding an animal

wild — not tame; found in nature

INDEX

acts, 30, 33, 34, 41, 45
animal cages, 5, 8, 17
animals, 8, 11, 14, 17, 18,
    20, 23, 30, 36, 37, 42, 45
animal tricks, 18, 20, 23, 37, 45
bands, 8, 33
big cats, 17, 18, 36
Big Top, 25
cages, 5, 8, 17
camels, 14
cats, 17, 18, 36
clowns, 40
cookhouse, 12
doctor, 42
elephants, 8, 11, 23, 37
giraffes, 14
horses, 20, 37
kitchen, 12
leopards, 17, 18
lions, 8, 17, 18
lion tamer, 36
motor homes, 5, 43

music, 33
parades, 8, 33
poles, 30
riders, trick, 20, 37
rings, 30, 34
rope, 26
seats, 25, 29, 41
sick animals, 42
tents, 5, 8, 11, 12, 25,
    29, 41
tigers, 17, 18
tightrope wires, 25, 30, 39
trailers, 43
trains, 7
trick riders, 20, 37
tricks, animal, 18, 20
    23, 37, 45
trucks, 5, 12, 14, 17, 43
wild animals, 17
winter home, 45
zebras, 14

About the Author

A long-time resident of Salt Lake City, Utah, Mabel Harmer was a teacher, and the author of juvenile stories that appeared in a local newspaper daily for more than ten years. The mother of five children and now a grandmother, Mrs. Harmer has practical knowledge about the wide range of subjects that interest young readers.